Syllables

&

Leaves

BY

WENDY SALOMAN

First published in 1997 by **Salzburg University** in its series:

EDITORS: WOLFGANG GÖRTSCHACHER & JAMES HOGG

ISBN 3-7052-0137-9

INSTITUT FÜR ANGLISTIK UND AMERIKANISTIK
UNIVERSITÄT SALZBURG
A-5020 SALZBURG
AUSTRIA

Distributed by
    Drake International Services
    Market House, Market Place,
    Deddington OXFORD OX15 0SF
    England
    Phone 01869 338240
    Fax N°: 01869 338310

Distributed in the U.S.A. by
    International Specialised Book Services Inc.
    5804 NE Hassalo Street
    Portland
    Oregon 97213-3644
    Phone 503.287.3093
    Fax: 503.280.8832

Syllables

&

Leaves

BY

WENDY SALOMAN

UNIVERSITY OF SALZBURG

SALZBURG - OXFORD - PORTLAND

Acknowledgements and thanks are due to *The Salmon Magazine* in which some of these poems first appeared, and to *Stride* for publishing passages from "Lyric" in the anthology of prose poems, *A Curious Architecture*.

A PREFACE, OR TEN QUESTIONS ANSWERED.

You asked me once whether I write or compose. May I begin by addressing you with your own question. Can you suggest the ways by which any of your poems evolve or come into being, whether you write to complete what's already written in the mind, or whether you proceed by impulse?

When I put the question to you I was reading Mandelstam, the poet who walked the streets composing his poems, who wondered how many sandals Dante wore out during the course of his poetic life wandering the goat paths of Italy, and who could not understand Pasternak sitting at his desk each day to write. So what is it, I had pondered, that liberates the internal rhythms necessary to the composition of poetry? Like many poets, I both compose in the Mandelstam sense and write in the Pasternak sense. The heightened awareness between lips, tongue and ear of the former is closer to the composition of music. My poetry usually comes into being by impulse. A feeling, perception or thought, finds its nearest correspondence in an image, then I look for all the sonority I can command from words and the process of building the poem begins. The relationship between sound and image is integral; they generate themselves and each other, assonance and alliteration interweave with the outer and inner eye. I think in terms of texture, but which is the warp and which the weft is difficult to say. The poem evolves, sometimes at the most surprising moments, as clusters of thought, sound and image emerge. More often than not there are many drafts. I can wait days for the precise word, the unexpected image can change the course of the poem, or it can be the one to conclude it. But a poem is not finished until the sound is right. The underlying structure of a poem, the moving force, once given shape, unifies experience, belief and need, and thus brings a fresh dimension of meaning to light. The act of writing has become for me the process towards that meaning, be it the pursuit of the transient, the affirmation of some moral order, or simply a greater understanding.

Although strongly musical your poems would seem to come from a painterly eye. Would you agree? And if so, to what degree would you be prepared to describe yourself as a poet of nature? Your work is full of birds, flowers and waves.

Just as poetry demands the attention of the ear, it demands the attention of the eye. Ruskin, who stimulated Proust's eye, stimulated mine. And to some extent, so did Rilke with his emphasis on seeing. The desire is to penetrate to the essence of things by visual perception. But there is a sense of disappointment for the writer because one cannot capture the immediacy of that perception with words. I have always thought that the relationship between the eye and the brush and the canvas is more direct than that between the eye, the word and the page. Yves Bonnefoy has interesting views about this in his poetics and essays on art. Many years ago I saw a small painting in the Tate Gallery, it was of gleaners in a field of light. I forget the name of the artist but I remember it was that of a woman. The scale of composition and the intensity of the light made a deep impression upon me as it seemed to disclose more than the physical light. I thought, this is what I want my poetry to do. I don't consider myself a nature poet as such, rather one who draws from it out of love, and in the belief that nature is where we are most in touch with our primal selves, therefore where we are most whole. I find living in a city, which I have always done, creates a great yearning for natural landscape, and as soon as I am in the country, or by the sea, I fill my notebook with repetitive jottings and observations. The potency of the word makes me feel I can bring nature back home, as I bring shells from the shore, fallen fir cones from the woods.

What immediately strikes the reader is the unEnglishness of your work, particularly in the use of the prose poem, a form that has never really caught on here. Would you say that your adoption of the prose poem is a conscious one, or, rather, has the subject demanded the form?

The subject began to demand the form, and then I found the form had a great deal to offer. I wanted to extend a narrative and theme, and of course I was taking the step from the very short poem. I needed to retain the poetic impulse, the charged language, and the sense of illuminating moments of perception, feeling, thought or experience.

You quote from St. John Perse and Edmond Jabès, both of whom have used the prose poem as their main vehicle. To what extent have you been influenced by them and by the German poet, Nelly Sachs?

St. John Perse and Edmund Jabès, two very different poets whom I have read with a similar reverence. But sometimes I think it is difficult to know how much or how little an influence has been. One reads and absorbs and then makes one's own way. The epigraph to "Canto" is from St. John Perse's *Amers*, a work I find quite marvellous in content and structure. I know of no other poet of the twentieth century who celebrates nature with such fecundity of imagination. The abundant language of the natural world and the correspondences of images create in themselves and through analogy and symbol an existential theme of unity and presence. A theme I am very drawn to.

Jabès, the poet of the self-perpetuating question of Jewishness and the Jewish experience, was immediately of interest to a quite other aspect of myself. I admire the fusion of imagination and enquiry. The drama of the letter, the metaphysics of the written word, the Book, are the themes of the Jewish tradition. But as a woman, and as a writer of a very different kind, he hovers in the Pale rather like the grandfather I never knew, but felt I knew.

Nelly Sachs has without doubt played a greater part in my life. When by chance I discovered her *Selected Poems* in the second hand department of Dillons' old university bookshop, I had found the author of poems with a vision and strength of feeling that resonated within myself. A felt affinity such as this with a greater poet can have its problems. One enters into her work and enters the enigmas of the universe. Her protest against, and lament for, the Holocaust is a cry of the soul against the violation to humanity when hate is the guiding principle. Her theme of metamorphosis is her faith, and that faith on the page is both mysterious and luminous; her language is that of love.

Rimbaud?

It's many years since I've read Rimbaud. Yes, his verbal alchemy and freedom of imagination marked my young mind. There is something about the French imagination, the surreality, intensity, whimsy? which has always appealed to me. Perhaps that accounts for some of the unEnglishness you speak of in my work.

Would it be true to say that you have also drawn on your sympathies with a Jewish culture, and, if so, how would you define that Jewishness?

I grew up with a love of English literature and accepted it completely as my heritage. But I think there is a Jewish sensibility, a

European Jewish sensibility is perhaps more accurate, and I have been faintly surprised to discover the extent of this sensibility in my own writing. It is there quite unconsciously. Hannah Arendt spoke of Jewishness as "an existential given". And Paul Celan on his visit to Israel in 1969, used one word to define his Jewish identity, "selbstverständlich" which translates into English as "understandable of itself". I don't think I could find a statement as succinct and encompassing as either of these to define what is almost impossible to define, and yet immediately makes one Jew recognise another. However, there are certain values which are deeply rooted and go so far back in time that even were one to shake them off they would return of their own volition. The Jewish spirit is one that endures, and it is loyal to its past even when it adopts its host's culture. Nor can it betray the history of Jewish suffering. At the time of the Holocaust I was a small carefree child, and I have often wondered what might have happened to myself and my family if the weather conditions had allowed Hitler to cross the English Channel.

Returning to St. John Perse and Edmond Jabès; were you suggesting you experience a conflict in what you find in the two different poets?

The presence of the natural world as evoked by St. John Perse and the presence of the word in Jabès 'Book' can take me in opposing directions, although ultimately to the one truth. The conflict is partially resolved in the activity of writing which enables us to hold contradictions as if in the palm of a hand. I think without such tensions we wouldn't write poems.

If there is a single sorrowful note in your work it is that sounding loss, whether it be of a parent, a love, or, indeed, of a value. Would you say that for you poetry is the reclaiming of that loss?

In the case of lost values, one cannot reclaim in the social and political sense; the poem remains a lament or admonishment. The reclaiming takes place in the inner life. My poem to Nathan Sharansky demonstrates this. As far as personal loss is concerned, the power of the word as a tool toward healing is great. Out of absence we bring presence. The nature of that presence I question in "Lyric" just as I question the illusion of presence we get from a photograph. "Bringing Forth Letters" has a debt to Heidegger's, "Calling brings closer what it calls". I had been reading *Language, Poetry and Thought* and the poem came into being. Of course it also contains Judaic allusions. In "Canto" I wanted to explore sorrow through a correspondence with the sea. The sea effects our psyche; how many times do we observe people looking at it as if they were drawing from it some essential part of themselves. The poem "In memoriam P.B." is simply that. I would say that in naming sorrow I bring a meaning to it that goes beyond itself.

How important is myth to you and how valid is it in a world which has become increasingly materialistic, a fact which seems to be reflected in much of the poetry which is being written at present?

Without the thematic thread of Isis and Aphrodite, of Eros and Mercury, "Lyric" would not have been written. The thread is the armature of the poem. When as a young person I discovered that the Greek word 'mythos' meant simply 'story', it was like opening a treasure chest from antiquity of eternal realities. Identifying with them the I becomes timelessly present and is part of universal experience. H.D., who made it her own, referred to myth as a kind of spiritual etymology. I became fascinated by the evolution of the goddess; Isis had many names, many functions, whereas in the Greek pantheon Aphrodite personified one.

A symptom of spiritual loss and excess materialism is that the ego becomes sovereign at the expense of all else (in a totalitarian society one could say the sovereignty of the ego is that of the state). This creates, inevitably, the alienation, the confusion of values, and the carelessness towards the earth, we witness today. Myth as the shared experience unifies, and in returning to its source we find corresponding patterns of the sacred throughout cultures. I wanted to place my story in the greater fabric of the gods.

A professor of mine said that the first question anyone should ask of a poet's work is who, what or where his God is. It seemed a strange question coming from one whose own god was politics, a god which I believe finally strangled his lyric voice. Whereas I cannot remember any of the poems he wrote his question has stuck with me. Certainly he was asking us to address the page; I am in the rather fortunate position of asking you what your God or god is?

To speak of unity, to speak of the sacred, is easier than to speak of God. Yet perhaps it is the same? To speak further of the Creator, the

Absolute, the First Principle, is to speak of a leap into hope because a meaningless universe is more incomprehensible. Therefore I believe in the necessity of God. But what kind of God this God of necessity is, remains forever a question.

Of the gods? Well, one of them urges me to write.

Interlocutor: Marius Kociejowski

SYLLABLES AND LEAVES

Canto
Shadowsound and Coda
Syllables and Leaves
Theme and Variations
Lyric
Bringing Forth Letters

Canto

> *Unité retrouvée présence recouvrée! O Mer*
> *instance lumineuse et chair de grande lunaison.*
>
> St.-John Perse.

The fulvous season: the wind of a fallen world wraps itself round the trees, scatters the tensile spores; the hush in the room is emptied of sleep.

Somewhere the sea is eloquent, ruthless; the light written over it like a covenant.

Once I pledged my cry to the waves, exalted.

Once by the water's rim the laughter of children remained.

You bring me the enigma of the rose. I sense in its centre the presence of death and fasten my old hands about yours.

Words tumble out of the dark unsuspecting of time's violence.

We journey through love and regret. Where you do not venture you imagine.

Thus we make up stories and words wait on us, the hand-maidens of myth.

Now I am with you, now I am not; the hour extends an arm into the past gathering moments, images.

Brine in my hair, butterflies amid wild blue scabia; celandine, nettles and a spider's web spun between foliage.

Some say Penelope wove with the thread of memory and that it had the resonance of aether.

Yes, a rapacious chaffinch pinked the early morning air, as if defending the territory of myth.

The river predicated the sound with an irregular measure; there, beside the stone walls of the house, sanctuary of my childhood.

A benediction of swans, and in the near distant light milky tongues rushed to the shore where algae covered small rocks thrusting into space like basilisks.

Movement of minutiae in pools, transfiguration of clouds —

I offer you this memory so you may cast a net into its transience.

Sometimes the river carried murmurings of the past, and the sun crept to rest in remembrance of the massacred. And when the sea-winds gathered their chromatic force, the vocabulary of the waves mingled with that of the dead; and the sea's swell became a great lectern frothing with the noise of history.

I turned to the narrative of stone, moon and shell —

But the weeping of the mourners flowed to my dreams.

Once I took you there, where the river surrenders its name to the sea. The summer was dense, lilting; hellebore skies filled with nostalgia; the sea-gods no longer mocked us. You were a child, in heart I was too.

The surface of the water glittered with the legends I told you: we waded like birds of joy.

Then I traced the wind of the future over the sand and you ran across the beach, desireless.

At the edge of your smile sadness raises a lamp to the evening. Tell me more, you say.

The dead are not dead.
I see her tired oval face in the fading light:
Come in to bed, she calls across the fields, her soft voice raised, the texture of the moist earth —
And the entire village sharpened its ears.
Timeless, I straddled my universe.
Later, I hid in her laughter's embrace; the sea washed the sands with rippling crescendos.
Now she stands at the brink of mornings, her laughter scattered.

Immense saffron light; space; gulls the screaming chroniclers of the sky; the sea the canto of my grief.
They took my mother's coffin into the church, placed oak on oak. We lit candles scented with life and knelt to the Intercessor of all Sorrows.
Tears reflected tears of estranged tides, landscapes in which I was as motionless as she was in death.
O Stellar Maris, hear us, we prayed. O rosary of endurance.
And the waves were gently monotonous, like those that bore Astarte to Greece.

We left footprints in the sand, our eyes the wells of expectation.
The boat bringing my father home appeared on the horizon, a funereal word emerging into the script of the sea.
The light and the particles of colour engraved a system of time like a dance.
He was captaining the grammar of the wind, folding his heart into her absence.

She was half-bird, half-woman.

He had imagined her giving herself to death; filled his lungs with the subtlety of her last breath.

With fire in his throat he sang of her.

And he remembered cities, ports, bays, and the promise of her voice always beside him.

The beach had been indolent with gold when he had placed her in his cage of love; the sea had rolled in with Homeric whisperings.

In our innocence we imbibed his story.

He said: You resemble your mother in the way a swallow leaves its shadow over water.

And as the birds dipped their wings in the vanishing light, I wanted to dig into the grave, take her hand, wrap it in the night sky until life re-entered.

Then in the beguilement of dream, I heard the hurdy-gurdy man with his Sunday delights.

She was dancing on the shore, refusing death; her eyes large, ravaged.

And the sea conversed with the sky, phrasing an incorruptible language.

Ah, the clownfullness of age; memory looking out of a dimly lit palace.

The architect of the joke smiles, but you who are young do not see it.

I tell you, he, also, had eyes the sea had entered, he who led me to the threshold of the gods.

I remember watching the moon exchanging its currency with the sea, counting the waves, measuring the constancy of love.

When the long violet arm of the evening holds up the weight of the sky and the day subsides into the sea, the bird in flight is perfection, he said.

Often I hear his voice disturbing the present with the movement of dream.

He wept with his whole body when I turned away; he who taught how to sow forgiveness in an unfertile land, and how to wait for the flower.

For when the sun leaves its last mark on the sky, the time of humility begins.

With the vigour of scribes the waves disclose remnants of the pain we have thrust each upon another.

As the water darkens the pilgrimage toward things past intensifies.

Prophetic shells, medusae, rocks pitted yellow and encrusted, witness a moment of resolution.

And the energy of the sea is tossed by the winds across the loneliness.

You speak to me of purity and wisdom.

Not pure. Not wise. But an old woman who still seeks herself in a flatterer's eye.

You chase after words forgetting it is the silences that bind us.

Immured, a fly drones.

It is not death I fear but the breaking of the branch at the edge of death's country.

Sometimes the night cries out for the homeland of childhood, for the invisible promises of dawn.

Death's emissary weighs the substance of longing against that of the hour.

Words drift over the river like leaves already crisp with silence.

The boatman has his hand on the oar, but the water reflects eyes unready for the passage.

Weightless in some nameless land I wake and watch the mobility of the shadows.

*

O shadowlands, where the dying converge —
Where the shattered throats are dry with suffering like grasses in an unsung desert —
Where all vibration is out of tune with the night and the sound of the stars is hidden —
Let in the weeping sea, the fugitive light; let in primordial memory.

*

She laid the syllables of the old woman's name on the sea and heard the chant of the requiem.
Seeking her in death she questioned the absence with the luminosity of a sun, and the coldness rose up to the fullness of meaning, there on the dark ebb of the tide.

Shadowsound and Coda

When through the trees the thrush
Makes its last offering to the day
Emptying light sharpens the ear —
And somewhere in the shadowsound
There is a granary of hope
Where immured thought may climb out of fear.

Ascending, January trees —
Through a field of thick air
To a clarity of language.
And we uproot words
Dealing them into nets.

Light in the eye of a needle flowers —
A song from an ancient root —
But tongues hammer leaves of fragility
And they will shoe Pegasus for death.

.

Petal by petal
The corolla of a world
Screams into the universe.
Once we heard it
Lullabied by the stars.

Red rowan, November day, a pale sun
Beats in a blackbird's breast. My fear —
That it will leave its holy ash, condemn
The earth beyond all fabled loneliness.

The burnt leaf off shore,
The last animal dying; black
Sand, black bone, an angel
Crying — black requiem.

The sun soaks into marrow —
The sky is the ancient's blue —
And bees in their hurry
Forget the flowers paling
From Azrael's night spinning.

Always the hope of saffron in the sky
And dawn's bursary of promises —
Only a tongue stumbles — fearing
Ashen words in a double-dealer's song.

In ochre and gold, imagine
Oriental hands weaving
Threads into blossom —
But do you hear the murmuring buds
Below the glow of the pattern?
Whose were the lips silenced by fear?
The honey made bitter —
The bee to be forgotten.

And with the bouyancy of light
axles shrieked over innocence.

You who murdered at the seventh gate —
The sun that reddened over Thebes
Reddens the earth seven times deeper —
There are those holding a curse in their hands
Who still hunt in the gullies of hate
For the light-threads of their inheritance —
And ears with patinas of grief
Cannot hear in the landscape of cries
The dead haunting humanity to its grave.

Once with smoke-black ink
They wove syllables of the law
Illuminating the delicacy of faith —
Then like great eagles
They hungered after letters —
Alienated them from their source.

Sharpening ineluctable cries
In a market-place where cruelty is cheap —
A knife-grinder confuses one with another.

You, the estranged, your callousness flowers
At the noon of obsession —
Grief for the violated ones
Glows in the terrible light
While the reflection of split gods
Quivers with clarity —
There, in the eyes of those
Ensnared like surprised doves.
You, the estranged
We would snow over your fear making
Prayerward with tears —
We would turn your hour into the nexus of night.

And in the dark province of the testimony
They thread the silence of tongues
For all utterance —
Blown by malevolent winds
Reverberates with the windrose —
Metronome amid the day's killing.
As if by the subtlety of a wasp
Memory flings up images —
The beacon of the dead flashes
Across the century's anguish.

But there, on the far edge of hate
Where the Erinyes shawl themselves in silence —
Music of leaves can be heard
In consort with voices of the dead —
And despair, thrust by grace into a bird of sorrow —
Soars above the earth where hell has too much light.

Syllables and Leaves

I want to bring to your eyes
The river where the swans
Measure the air of your childhood —
Then let the hours in your hands
Speak with the silence of Rembrandt.

I want to catch the light
In which your humbleness glows
And return it to the cliffs of your sadness.
I want to find in December trees
Prayer for the weigher of souls
And for the ears of Rhamiel, birdsong.

Old woman, you sleep, and day and night
Frailty sleeps with you
Waiting unwanting for the pearl of your death.

Not the vision of Constantine,
Not the joy in the throat of the angel —
The sanctus of the Tuscan's palette
Celebrates its laws behind a closed window —
And we, at the edge of the mystery,
Mingle in the Arezzo choir
With butterflies of light
Crushed by the syllables of Babel.

But you, conciliating grief
On the branches of kinship
Were strung beyond time
Negating Creon's edict.
Suspended between silence
And language, eternally law —
Love, childstemmed, memory-rooted,
Tuned your light to the light of the dead.

*The tears shed for a good man are taken
into heaven and stored there as gold.*

Grief is the willow
Wintering our tears —
Falling where death
Is the bird made stone.

Blessed are the eyes
Weeping snow into blossom —
Beyond us a tree
Sheds songs of your gold.

for A.

1

As a fabulous beast thrusting
Out of a dark throat of laughter —
The child in the dying garden
Questions the sun and the earth.

How she moves into her own mythology,
The child in the red dress —
Dancing an imagined trepak
Lured to the mirror
Cunningly transmuted.
How she tosses the head
Stemmed from a siren
And laughter and ache
Measure power fearing failure —
My daughter, my angular tulip.
How guarding the leaves
I stumble serving her empire
Caught by demand and guilt
And reflection in the mirror —
Moving myself
In the heart of her hand.

3

And doves I number
Counting you to sleep
Child of the foxish day —
For betrayal drifts
In the ebb and flow of dream
To shores of lunar clarity —
And there shells speak
Of the providential bird
Dipping its branch again and again
In a world's sea of tears.

4

O eyes, landscapes of dusk,
O tears, opaque lakes —
O fish dizzy with words
You gamble as you swim between shores.
O world of rippling enigmas —
Can the night-fisherman know
How to make the moonlit catch
As stars into a miraculous net?

Winter day dying — the heart's matter;
Children at the sun's edge of the common —
Nothing new, feelings and fallen leaves
As little gods cry and the women appease.

The still-hour,
The blackbird —
And heart-split
I barter for time.
But in the market
Creeps anxiety —
The sand-thief
Diminishing the song.

That it should come tenderly in the night
Weeping and thornless
When the flowers speak softly of your life.
That it should take perfectly the worn heart
Ploughed-up with light
While wrapped in sleep your fear is weightless.
That it should sing with the birds of the law
Of love and daughter —
The enigma binding us in your last hour.

Uprooted,
Borne into the crevice
Of a wind-swept smile,
A language of pain —
And there
Quietly you blossom,
Adamant in the light
Of your unshed tear.

Hollow eyes — the night's disease,
The coming and going of the mind
A shopkeeper's paradise. Between stars
An amulet falls as an evening primrose.

This brittle leaf in my hand,
This hour of cinnamon closing,
This landscape of doubt
Lingering with self-accusation:
This tremor of flight,
This shrill of starlings fading,
This day, this I
Falling to silence and decreation.

for Nathan Sharansky.

And when you inscribed the bitter air
You tuned the Hebraic heart
By its root-light
Nurtured there in the psalms —

With breath from your song an evening bird
Broke open the dusk
As if promising a blossoming of letters —

Night rode toward you
Vibrant with the longing —
The moon threw back
Remembrance of each exile
Journeying on the map of their endurance.

And where in your nocturnal lungs
Did the death-boat break apart
And leave the last breath perfect?
Unutterable dominion
This premature midnight —
Oceanic, bare of birds, violent.

Or did the anguish of the sun
Blaze the last hour of frailty?
We willed you the gentle light
Behind the eye of the narcissus —
Dared you to take the leap —

Now, the geography of your smile
Joins us in one body of grief —
We recollect it rushing from eyes
Across the fertility of your cheeks —
Within the smile, recognition —
Behind, the mile-down glimmering of angst.

You calculated the clarity of a life
With boyish enthusiasm
Gravely measuring the elements
In your sceptic's universe.
One day, in this world, you said —
We may be bodiless light
Exchanging infinities —
Time no longer consuming us with fire.

But like a bespoke dream
In some humming forest
Heavenward oak was felled for a coffin —
When the priest opened the funereal doors
To sun on leaves and resonant crocus
We wept the copper tears
You would offer as a coin to the ferryman.

There, in the blue of your eye
Was a dwelling place for the tear.
You told me she had walked to death
Willing the ripples of her own destruction
Burnt out as the palest flower.
You had smelt the centre of yourself in her —
You, who were afraid to die into love
And in dying found it in abundance.

Eyeing the world, you praised —
But when anger looked on anger
A blindfold beast tore at your body.
I imagine breathless cypresses —
The silence of swallows
Disclosing all that is transitory
In a phenomenal light.
And I hear you rage about your voyage.

Be still. We know no justice.
I fill my pen
With the dread of the living —
From some kind of hell
You climbed into the emptiness before us —
Your voice here in my heart.
O the metamorphosis of ash
When light returns to light.

Noon-blest, the tree waits for its fruit
And the earth quivers
As it receives the ash —
Can you hear yet
The blossom celebrating your death?
The dead are the light-bearers —
Their laws are the laws of pure song.

Ungraspable. Your absence —
Like a rare bird
Darting through density of matter —
We leaf your life-tune
In the fluctuation of memory.

I search the sky for images —
Remembering we toboganned in its snow
And the purity of winter
Alchemized our laughter.
Clouds form words we argued over for hours —
We thought, then, we knew their meaning —
We didn't weigh them
As the Egyptians weighed the hearts of the dead.

I open my sadness as if it were a book —
Words judge me as I judge them —
Between the syllables and leaves
Creases of your smile hunt me out
Where my fidelity fell short
In an unwanted country of the past.
I am earthed in the same vanities —
Measure me now as you will.

Primeval, the eye of the anemone
Absorbs the silence of light.
Vibratile —
Gesticulating grace
The festal flesh uncurls
And the hegemony of colour
Burgeons into dance —
Like a wind-woven script
Before the ages of grief.

As a thief, the lonely hour
Broods in the throat
Until the sharp edge of yearning
Hews from the silence an octave of light —
Briefly fear glows
And from my pen the letters unfurl
Like birds of passage travelling homewards

Theme and Variations

Ashen
Where light shatters on water
Gulls pledge their cry —
And I take your name
From the root of the willow
Conjuring up seconds of memory
Of you
Entering my senses —
You, the blazing god of the blood.

No wife but wanting, I, stemmed from Rachel,
Wait with stars fertile outside your window.
And you, quiet orient, within heart's reach,
Unable to measure the dust in the breeze.
How it blinds eyes between garden and house.

Threshing waves — I angle our day's experience —
Moonlit the minnows dart mercurial — and sombre
A world winces. I long for grey-eyed dawn, rose
Of vision. Beside me you lie locked — silently
Grieved and doubting a shrew's intolerance.

Needlepoint of loneliness — the opaque
Eye weeps and blames, deposits venom —
And seeps into paper domes of domesticity.
O to build this love a city of granite.

Blinded, Narcissus stumbles
Amid flaming petals at noon.
Love, sweep the ash from the earth —
Restore the eyes seeking otherness.

And black with night, two birds
Fasten to the summering branch —
Breast to breast they bruise
Their song confused and painlit.
Quietly into the leaves of dawn
Heart revoke the childroot blame —
It is we bound by the wounds we know
Who must plough our star-bled images.

Desire, as willow leaves fall,
As sparrows empty their sound
And our understanding quivers,
Flowers on tongues of discontent.

Only the sound of the crickets
And the smell of the charred earth
As a leaf falls flaming
Into Medusa's cold hand.
O imperial month, under your sky
Aeons of paradox have passed across lips —
He I desire moves now
Only stone in the eye of our heart.

Burning the tongue, burning the heart,
Death flowers delicate as the earth's
Last crocus. O kill, comes a cry —
Love is over. Who? is the reply —
My roots are bound to ash and gardener.

The wound opens an eye —
The word rises —
And a crocus returns
From Aphrodite's embers.

And out of the stillness into the worn
Gold eye, gulls cry over the river, heart
Carriers returned from a planetary gutter —
Sound redeemed, our key no longer bitter.

Unshadowed unfolds the hour —
Its drift, seafarer,
Taking us to the sanctuary
In the wells of our eyes.
Anchored on breath —
Crepuscular words
Fear to unsilence the light.

In the movement of your face
The fall of snow, the sorrow,
Each flake an absence
Measuring our negation.
Yet in the silent space —
Still between suns,
You, unknowing your shadow,
Guard divinity grave as a child.

Luminous the winter trees —
As an order of priests
Blessing icebitten words —
Time bruised to be healed —
And into the light — our eyes.

Lyric

The very fact of the shadow of the person
lying there fixed forever ...
                    Elizabeth Barrett Browning.
          Letter to Mary Russell Mitford, 1843.

Ach! Wir kennen uns wenig,
     Denn es waltet ein Gott in uns.

Ah, ourselves we know little,
     For within us a god commands.
                         Hölderlin.

1

Violets were the death-flowers of the Greeks.

They were the flowers of love, you said. And you put some into my hand as a gift from the gods.

God-flowers, flowers of grace, their petals are darkened by clairvoyancy, I said.

The eye of your camera closed on the violets, impressing their ephemeral image into grains of silver.

With all the subtlety of the messenger of the gods, the camera strikes a bargain with time, and an image is made into shadow and remembrance.

In the drawer of a mahogany desk (amid the chaos of old experience) I have kept the photograph of the violets, together with the one I took of you soon after we met.

I caught you in a field of summer grasses, contemplating the geometry of the green and ochre blades. I caught the breath of the day; the sun on your lips; your ears attentive to the hum of the earth; the texture of the sky in a butterfly's wings; the texture of your clothes, the immaculate whiteness of cotton, the fine twill of grey wool. I caught the birth of a moment consecrated with joy.

I look now at the image which is you and not you.

Quixotic: contrary. Shyness and humour in the pull of your Anglo-Saxon eyes.
Can remembrance revivify the reality of experience?
Can I conjure presence from shadow?

4

The photograph of the violets has begun to curl at the edges. You had found them in the snow that winter which had lingered through March.

We were obsessed with omen and discovery; with the past and future present in the force of Eros.

The sun's constancy to the snow, the flaming close to surprised days, gave clarity to our senses and to the power we gave to words.

You are the eternal mystery of woman, you said.

You, who are a Hebrew, left roots in Egypt with Isis.

Imagine Isis collecting fragments of her dead Osiris.
Imagine collecting fragments of our life together.
Imagine hearing our voices from the past.

Imagination is the instrument of eternity.

Once, we discovered from an ancient text that souls descended to earth through your constellation, through mine they ascended to heaven; they were named the Gate of Men and the Gate of the Gods.

So the crab and the goat are eternal partners in the play and the dance.

The absurd and the tender mingled in your words.

I will always love you. All ways at all times.

We made our vow in the room in the white Victorian house.

To remember the room is to remember any room with the morning light through thin curtains, light on white sheets, light on clothes thrown over chairs.

We dream in this room, you said. We dramatize ourselves; we are naive and arrogant; we have vision and fear.

And in the room Eros was the fire of the alchemists.

Each sanctuary of love has its laws and rituals.

We dined at a table where I worked during the day, dined amidst words revealed and hidden.

Above our heads a cheap Cézanne print vibrated with colour; apples charged with feeling transcended weight and time. I remember thinking, we project this colour, feeling, timelessness, into the room.

Time made you timid. The ebony clock on the mantelpiece reminded you of all that was not yet done.

You found time in the vase of flowers next to the clock.

Time was carved in an oriental bird of jade; time was in pebbles and shells brought home from shores. We beautified time, ignored time, transcended time, but still you said, Time presses on ruthlessly, and we must be as ruthless as time.

How can I remember the room without remembering your absence?

A collection of postcards and letters from all parts of the world preserved the mark of your absence. They were written with love, guilt, care, haste; they always expressed ambivalent thoughts on your mercantile travel; they always expressed the spirit of Eros in absence.

(Eros in absence was our weakness and our strength.)

You wrote on a postcard from Greece, Here are some stones to adorn the mantelpiece.

And from Egypt you wrote, The death of the sun here is an erotic hymn. Do you remember the winter of the violets?

I answered, I remember the violets and the smell of the pine needles; I remember the crocus beneath the snow; I remember death and regeneration.

Remembrance washes over your image like the play of light on water. Yet as I reflect on the elusive expression in your eyes and how you hid your laughter from the camera, the midnight is blue; amorphous clouds move rapidly over the full moon.

Was the moon at its height over Magdalen Tower?

Was it as luminous as memory?

We had returned to where memory is stored in turrets and spires; where intellectual dreams compete with gargoyles mocking each other line by line, face to face; the absurd and the grotesque reminding us of imagination's place.

We had returned to where the bustle of a universe emanates from stone.

I remember you said, I wasted my days here. I wish I could have them again. And the cloister of the college absorbed your words as if someone spoke them there year after year, age after age.

We had followed the past wherever it whispered; across quadrangles and perfect lawns; in ragwort, marsh-marigolds; in grasses of water-meadows, in the river banked with limes.

We had heard the chant of centuries before the rising of the moon.

And then we had paid homage to Her river.

The moon was your ruling planet, your emblem a shell.
(The sea spoke in your bones, your dreams, your lust.)
We met by the sea.
We summered in a vortex, unable to measure the space between uncertainty and joy.
Waves broke on rocks. Milk of seduction was tossed into the air.
Cézanne called Helios the painter of the universe, you said, as we watched the evening light on water.
We watched fields and furrows of purples and browns, yellows and greens, spawning amber pools, and the thin violet bar separating sky from sea.
I thought, if I could catch a seagull I could catch time.
We watched the sun emptying the wound of the day; the transformation of the water to a cloth of cream-gold across an even pale grey. The deepening violet died into the sea, while upward the sky turned mauve, upward to the cumulus, to the cirrus, upward until it merged into a pale white-blue: this colour, this space, we thought, is where all desire meets and is satisfied.
Then we turned away from the swoosh of the waves; from the twilight and the hovering insects and the leaves trembling on the apple tree; from the celebration of the moment we had wanted to be eternal.

Summers were often full of spells, meetings and partings, tender reconciliations.

Life is not tender, you said, it is we who must put tenderness into life.

I had plunged into your eyes as I would into the sea.

I had committed myself to you believing the god would preserve the balance.

We loved the potential in ourselves.

We wrote our names on the palimpsest of the sea, and the letters reflected in each other.

We are all mirrors, and Eros is the illuminator of mirrors.

It is strange to remember the intimacy of hands: nurturers, explorers, instruments attendant on the word.

I caught the light in your hands and turned it into shadow in a field where an old ash had been felled.

Like Isis with her ameliorative fingers, the ash has healing power at the tips of its branches.

Did I unearth this folklore in a dream?

You wrote me once from Finland, The nights are long here; I miss the light from your fingers, but I catch it in my dreams.

I listen to Sibelius, I replied, and hear in his music the rhetoric of darknesses and light; of birds plummeting from geometrical flight into the brooding obbligato of Finland.

And I hear frailty in the hand of the poet who wrote, "I saw that the temple of Eros was made of human bodies."

Some say the camera is the instrument of death.
So, the hand that murdered resurrects!
And I journey into my past along the dead branches of the tree that will blossom tomorrow.

Was it chance or fate?

You said we met by chance, random as the wheel of roulette bewitching you that night.

Bizarre flunkeys opened door after door of gilded oak as I stormed out leaving you to babbling gods of fortune.

Not enough, you had said, I don't love you enough.

(Was it that I couldn't sustain your projection, your dream?)

Trouville was an echo of splendour. Gold-dust harboured in decaying stucco; exotic green paper peeled from walls. Facades that bronzed and purpled in the evening sun, dazzled in the whiteness of the morning. The municipal palace, designed by the architect to a pious dethroned king, lorded the seafront smelling of scandal and nostalgia.

Nostalgia was in the smell of the salt from the sea, in the timbers of the wide promenade, in the patterns made by the wind across the sand.

And here, you said, Boudin captured the breeze in the Empress Eugénie's hair.

And here, I said, the old man of the sea transformed himself into a shell like the one I hold to my ear.

And here, we said, nostalgia glitters even in the rain.

Nostalgia converges in your image.
What do I seek after all these years?
An ordering of experience? Or a language which travels toward revelation?
I remember. I imagine.

Rain and shadow fell across your face.

A drama was played out between the grey moving clouds and the yellow light. In the tensile moment before the liquid filaments entered the sea, the beach emptied into a vast silver waste.

Back in our faded room in the small pension, we drank wine and read Flaubert.

And here, I said, young Flaubert discovered his ever lasting love for Élisa Schlésinger.

You smiled into my glass.

In the silence I suddenly heard the mutterings of love's petty lies.

After the rain, the hushed world waited to be created again.

We opened our window, breaking iridescent threads of a spider's web.

It is fate, we said.

The fragrant smell of the tamarisk tree drew Isis to Byblos.

Once we made love under a tamarisk tree, and the stars invited us to share the fertility of their light.

When we destroy those we love, pain blinds us.

Often we would place demands upon each other knowing they could not be fulfilled.

You were negated by my fantasy, and I was reflected in your negation.

I remember the cries of the seabirds as they wheeled in the night space above us.

You said, I will always remember you, for you are all women.

There are moments in April when the cobalt sky is the heart's emissary.

When the blossom, thick and heavy on the trees, emits perfume and promises.

When the impregnable stillness at noon is close to perfection.

Perfection is an idea, you said.

(You never relinquished the idea; returning like the phoenix to possibility.)

Is perfection the death we experience in the photograph?

And some say Mercurius is the spirit of the camera and photography a form of alchemy.

A chymical marriage. A moment perfected and immortalised.

Mercury. Eros. A culture separates the sound. But a theme is congruent between the two.

When the Romans latinized Hermes, they rooted him in merchandise and trade.

God of merchants, light of alchemists, messenger of the ways of the gods, you are the trickster, the eternal *puer*, like Eros.

One night you dreamt you had buried your child.

Not our child. It was yours. But in the morning my grief was there in your eyes.

Time presses on, you said. We are victims of time yearning for eternity. Where is eternity in the death of my child?

You were to be haunted by the child.

For some years after we parted, I would imagine meeting you in some street or square with a small child's hand in yours.

It was a day of innocence and bright autumn sun when you told me she was carrying your child.

I avoided your eyes, your lips, but I was imprisoned by your anxiety and guilt.

I heard you say, We are friends, let us always be friends, all ways at all times; this doesn't have to make any difference to us.

Confession was cool air on your tongue.

Honesty and self-deception stared each other out.

Timeless, measureless, jealousy flowers into this world.

Daily, it extends a fugue through the universe.

One morning I observed the green leaves turning yellow. I thought, the earth is turning, my life is turning.

September was a month busy with preparations for your autumn travels.

Rowan berries flamed in the London streets; desire was tinged with sadness; starlings chorused valedictions beneath the cinnamon sky; and when evening brought us together, we put aside the contradictions of our lives.

We made silence an art.

Isis, they say, was once named the first of the Muses.

Isis whose names cannot be numbered.

Isis the patron divinity of travellers, the star of the sea.

Isis who personified all the mysteries of woman.

Isis whose rose was the flower of pure passion, the promise of immortality.

(Violets were the emblem of Athens, the flowers of Aphrodite: their intensity was their prophecy of death.)

Sometimes I went with you on the start of your journey; to Ostende, or to Bruges.

Once there was a sand-storm, and Nature seemed bent on destroying Herself. Sand blew into our hair, into our bones, over driftwood, debris, seabirds lying dead.

Years later, I dreamed of the sea at Ostende, of the sand-storm, whiteness, and an Egyptian scarab emerging from the sand. It was carved of carnelian when I took it in the palm of my hand, but when I put it in my mouth it tasted of blood.

"O my heart, the most intimate part of my being! Do not stand up against me as a witness before the Tribunal."

Thus wrote a scribe on a heart-scarab; a spell from the Book of the Dead.

And I swallowed the hieroglyph.

Bruges, city of bridges, Venice of the North, also called Bruges-la-Morte.

Copper leaves on their way to death shimmered in the canals.

City of swans; city of reflections. Articulations of the past, spires, turrets, red brick gabled houses, merged into infinite colour and form in the moment of the light on water.

City of Eros, imaged in water. Not with the dreaming decay of the Venetians, but with the purity and devotion of the Flemish. Forever minted in the spirit of medievalism, celebrating its merchants, weavers, chivalry; city of wool, city of the sea, its romantic fusion spoke to the essence of the dreamer in you.

But the mystery of Bruges was the enigma of faith reflected in water.

When, in the Groeninge Museum, we contemplated *Our Lady of the Sorrows*, you said, The heart of Bruges is in her slender hands. She is the eikon of absolute tenderness in grief. She who is the prayer, the perfection, the amen.

We walked through Bruges like pilgrims between syllables of faith.

We walked along narrow streets and quays, across bridges, past the working market, past the lacemakers, into the hour of chimes from the Belfry.

And we walked to the place they had named the Quay of Mirrors. We wanted to see how the sand, the death element of Bruges, had brought the canal to its close there.

You said, Bruges is like a poem, its theme is beauty and death.

I said, Beauty makes us yearn for eternity. Eternity illuminates death.

Memory with the pace of a summer regatta clutters the Heraclitean river.

Inevitably, we are estranged by flow and change.

Yet the past irradiates the present.

As I glance in the mirror, I see the Fates spinning in the pupils of my eyes: I see a young girl and a middle-aged woman. I see the one you loved, and I see in the one you loved all women.

Last night you surprised me in a dream.

I was standing by a window watching the shadow of the Woman of Troy. She was in Egypt taking refuge in a temple of Isis.

Some say Aphrodite created an image; an illusion started the war.

Emblems of Isis and Aphrodite overflowed into the dream.

Then marshland and papyrus silvered in a crepuscular light. From nowhere, a fantastic creature fell dead in its own pool of blood.

And, as if I were Helen, I dipped my hands into memory and wept.

Your voice vacillated between humour and gravity, punctuating the lyric.

Illusion, you said again and again, is like the foam of the sea. We need illusion. Illusion is need.

We needed ourselves in each other's eyes, enjoyed the images, until the illusion died. Simply, like the slip of the tongue from Eros to Eris.

Words leap into the mind, disappear, unshaped fragments of eternal experience.

Schubert and the blackbird are the unrivalled masters of variations on a theme, you said.

Music was light in our ears, in the swelling buds, in the red bark of tall pines; in your hand in mine.

And tuned beyond language, we entered into myth.

Bringing Forth Letters

The letters of the alphabet are contemporaries of death.
Edmond Jabès.

I see you stirring in death —
There beneath the wintered-through trees.
An arm extends toward the early sun —
The faint throb of flowers
Begins to resemble a heartbeat.
You spell out the word love —
I thread remembrance
Into the generosity of spring —

Calling you, the last wave of sound
Returns to the involuntary silence.
Starlings took your chatter into the sky
Coloured the cloud with syllables —
Those you had made into your book of hope —
Then, before the dawn of your dying —

Once I tore your words apart
Buried them in the space
Where the heart is still child —
Ah, but words endure, you had said
And where the air is soft with forgiving
Yes and No may reside together
Almost double-edging a butterfly's wings.

And bringing forth letters
Out of that fading storehouse
You form the words dark and light
As if they were your own creation.
Shadow plays in the room.
A January bird disturbs the air.
Your hand flutters into mine
Here, on its descent to death —

But there where the enigma
No longer guards its mystery
You run shadowless as a young girl
Nubile amid the yellow grasses.
The lilt of your voice is in my ear —
I arrest it with all its unspent passion.
Between your birth and mine
I hear the music of myth.

Like Deborah beneath the stars
Your heart rides the dark for life —
But your hair is white as the summit of death —
Your hands reach for the last green branch —
Summer could not dry the tears
You weep at the idea of surrender —
With broken speech you name your love for the earth —

Miraculously you play your last card
Close to the water's edge
In the presence of the ferryman —
Already your absence hums in the night —
Fear has gravitated toward you
Luminous as the moon celebrating your life.

And how easily death raises its voice
Here in the glory of the cherry blossom —
Faceless, it sings of you —
You who tried to efface it
With all the subtleties of fear
Until deception was knifed in the air —
Quivered, like the leaf I take from the tree —
Like the earth on its painful axis.

Dying, you wake to remembrance
So all that was once unhealable —
Unsayable, may be hammered into shape
Like leaves of gold —
For I have read fragments of your life
In the immense landscape
Now diminishing in your eyes —
Entered myself reflected there —

And in the name of the child
I recall the blossoming of nights —
Speak of Brahms and the promise of sleep —
Your agitated fingers then winged
On light across piano keys —
Tenderness in the universe,
Death's lullaby not yet sung.
And in the name of the child
Your fleeting smile remembers —

I recall the smile you threw away
The night of the unleavened bread —
I recall the glow behind your eye
When the herbs were bitter —
There in the room dense with the noise of custom
I heard the story of the tear
Waiting for the hush, waiting for Elijah.

You said the wind through the trees
Named the winterward soul.
Imprisoned by the tyranny of age
You no longer remembered its touch on your skin
As if it were the music of love
To be played on a heavenly instrument.
With Hebraic yearning
You unharnessed your loneliness.

Our voices cast by anguish into shadows
Pools from which you drink
For you hear clearly the words we speak —
And as each letter brings forth
The resonance of some familiar landmark
The response on your lips
Inscribes itself on the parchment of dying —

Now, consoling, the language of all things
Accompanies your breath
On its journey to the threshold —
There where the bird of the blood
Is unwinged among shattering images —
Where the flowers give themselves to the hymn of death —
And the hour climbs out of the night —
And the candles tune to the sabbath —

As if with the quiver of the psalms
Death overleaps dying
And love unfolds its law of fertility —
Soon children will sing out
And the potent play of letters will mingle
With the unforgotten words of the dead —
With the unshadowed silences
Strung like your name
To the narrative of the earth.

Heartstored, the ravaged petals of the rose
That with laughter you once called life.
Your hard dying was illuminated —
Now earth embraces you without passion.
With the fire of my breath I transform the word death.

Up-borne by the night's sap
Grief flows to the branch
Where the yellow bird
Communes with the coming light —
Yes, there in your absence
The twittering of metamorphosis —
And somewhere the constellation M
Changes its form and is named Mourning —

And there in the immeasurable place
Beyond the last beacon of fear
You have thrown off all syllables of longing
And the glimmer from your lips
Enters the songdrift of the no-thing beginning.
Amid leaves, amid shadow
I dream of fugue and remembrance
Taking from death your resolute cry —
And your hands bear festive fruit,
Your hair is as rich as the earth.

So many berries reddening on the trees,
So many leaves blown by the wind toward humus —
Autumn is passing over the dead.
Time for the memorial words to gather —
Time for the letters of your name
To regenerate with all that you praised.
Time for the so many shadows to draw ears closer
To the babble between fear and the unreachable stars.

Notes

Shadowsound and Coda

Page 19   Azrael is the Hebrew angel of death and destruction
Page 22   "You who murdered at the seventh gate"
           refers to *Seven Against Thebes*, Aeschylus.

Syllables and Leaves

Page 29   The weigher of souls is St. Michael. In Christian angelology
           he is the benevolent angel of death in the sense of deliverance
           and immortality.
           Rhamiel is the angelic name of St. Francis of Assisi. One of
           his roles is that of the angel of mercy.
Page 30   "Not the vision of Constantine" —
           The poem refers to Piero della Francesca's frescoes at the
           church of San Francesco at Arezzo.
Page 32   Epigraph: the words of Solomon according to an old Midrash.
Page 43   When Sharansky was arrested his wife sent him a small. book
           of psalms in Hebrew. It was confiscated, and in protest
           Sharansky went on strike. Consequently he suffered over 100
           days in the punishment cell. The book was finally returned to
           him. He later declared that the psalms had brought him nearer
           to his wife, family and people.

Lyric

Page 82   The Finnish poet, Edith Södergran (1892-1923), translated by
           David McDuff, 1984.
Page 94   Sappho describes Aphrodite as the 'Violet-breasted daughter
           of Kronos'.
Page 95   To the Egyptians the scarab symbolised the perpetual renewal
           of life.

Page 96   *Our Lady of the Sorrows* was painted by the school of Rogier
           Van Der Weyden (1399-1464).
Page 98   The source of the myth of Helen in Egypt seems to be the
           poet, Stesichorus of Sicily, a contemporary of Sappho.
           Euripides took up the story, and H. D. used the theme for her
           poem, *Helen in Egypt*.

Bringing Forth Letters

Page 107   "that bright, shining M,
           it stands for the Mothers." Rilke, *Duino Elegy* 10.